Tiana Tells:

A Guide to
Getting and Keeping a Man

ISBN- 13:978-0692081365

ISBN- 10: 0692081364

Congratulations on the purchase of this book. By buying this guide you are confirming that you are dedicated to trying to get or keep your man! If you are looking for Mr. Right, I believe reading this book is another way to use the power of manifestation to get what you want. You are putting your desire to find that special person out in the universe and when the time is right, you will get the perfect man and hopefully use some of the takeaways in this book to help keep him. I hope that you find this information useful be it reiterating things you may already know, or if I'm putting you up on game for the first time.

Some of you may wonder who am I, or why should you listen to what I have to say, right? Well I am just a woman with lots of insight because of my life experiences. I am a wife and mother to five beautiful children, but please understand that I have worn many different "hats" at different times in my life. I've been that young sexy girl with no kids, I've been the naïve girlfriend head over heels in love with a low down cheater (more than once). I stupidly accepted the role of a side chick before and sold myself completely short. I have also been a single mother, and a mother just playing house with my baby daddy who would constantly pressure him to get married all to no avail.

If I can help other women it would make me feel good. I would feel like all the heartache that I had to endure wasn't in vain. I mean I know it wasn't in vain because it made me who I am today and I wouldn't be such a good wife had I not lived a little before. I just want any woman reading this book to know that you are beautiful, you are worthy of love, and that you deserve the best. So with that being said if you are a reading this and it just so happens that you're on an involuntary penis fast because you just can't find a man, do not hesitate to take notes.

Table of Contents

So let's get to the good stuff!

First and foremost, you cannot keep a man who don't want to be kept. Please don't waste your time on a lost cause. Try to get with a guy who wants the same things as you. If the two of you actually click, then it should be smooth sailing. You won't have to go around trying to drop subtle hints. The proposal that you so desire will just happen naturally in due time. My husband, James, understood that he would never fully have me until he took that next step and put a ring on it. When we first started to date I told him, "I'm twenty-eight years old and I feel like I'm too grown to be somebody's girlfriend."

Because I had failed long term relationships in the past, I didn't respect the girlfriend title and being introduced as someone's "girlfriend" really got on my nerves. Until I said " I do," I had made up in my mind that I was going to keep my options open. The fellas were always choosing and as a single woman if I wanted to find out what one had to offer then I would. Let's be clear though, I was not having sex with multiple men at once. I would however, meet up for drinks or dinner to see if I was feeling them or where their heads were at. Lucky for James, no one made me feel the way he did so I stayed true and it worked out. Ain't God good?

At the end of the day there is no magic trick or one special thing I can tell you to do in order to get a man to exclusively date you or want to marry you. But a surefire way to increase your chances on getting a guy and making it down that aisle is to establish early on that you are not looking for a man who is only after a good time and not ready to settle down in the near future. Let it be known that you are hoping to get married in x amount of time and if he's not looking to do the same anytime soon then…have a nice life, it's on to the next! Don't think you have some magic va-jay-jay that's going to make him change his mind. If a man isn't ready to commit or get married, he simply is not going to do it.

Now just because you gave a disclaimer on your first date and he asked you out on a second one, that doesn't mean you should go buying up all the wedding books at Barnes and Noble. This is where you date and get to know him. Things still may not work out but you have increased your chances by putting it all out there from the jump. Unfortunately, there are some guys who are just not nice human beings and will lie and say that they too want to get married and start a family, just to get in your panties. This is where you will have to use discernment and trust your gut. More importantly, take things slow while paying attention to his actions. If he is texting you sweet nothings all day long while you're working but gets missing in the evenings, that could be a sign. Maybe he is unavailable in the evenings because he is at home with his woman and you should do a little further digging before you invest too much of your time. Basically if he says one thing but his actions are saying something different, then don't set yourself up for failure. The best way to get and keep a man is to make sure that you pick a good one from the start. This is where you have to believe in that woman's intuition that we all have.

Be careful of the type of guys you entertain and pay attention to the way you feel when you're around them because the universe will give you signs as well. If a man has multiple baby mamas or he isn't taking care of his kids, you should run, fast. Being a deadbeat is unacceptable and I don't care how crazy he claims his baby mama acts. Nothing would keep a man from his kids if he wanted to be in their lives. Clearly we are not talking about a real man so don't bother trying to change him. I know you are probably great but don't flatter yourself, you don't have the power to fix him. When dealing with a guy like this your credentials or how many karats of gold you think your coochie is made of means nothing! If he is just no good, then you are wasting your time. The sooner you can recognize a good for nothing loser, the better off you will be. If he is a dog he will roam and cheat on you just how he did the woman, he had before you.

Love is a gamble. You just have to take a chance. But you can increase your odds and possibly spare getting your feelings hurt if you don't get emotionally attached too soon. And remember that everybody you think you can vibe with a little bit don't deserve to have your body. Wait, save yourself, and really try to get to know these men before you give yourself to them completely and have regrets about it later. Sex feels great but regret feels Whore-able! So just think before you act please.

If you want a love like you've never had before, then sometimes you may have to do things for the sake of love that you've never done before. Let's say that you have trust issues and never fully gave anyone your heart or your trust. If your relationships haven't been working then maybe this time around you should be all in. For the first time in your life try letting your guard down, tearing down that wall, and trusting someone with your heart. You can do it. Also try turning and pointing the finger at yourself sometimes and try to figure out if there is anything that you are doing wrong that's causing your relationships not to work. If it is, then do what you can to better yourself.

BE CONFIDENT

Have you ever saw a girl who may be considered overweight, or may not have the best body but still knows how to walk into a room and totally own it? I have and when I see people like that I always admire their confidence. While I may consider myself to be a sexy little vixen now, when I was young I was skinny and flat chested. I remember in middle school I would hate when the kids would start talking about who was crushing on who or who had a nice body because it always led to a few of the guys turning their attention on me and starting with their "jokes". There was one boy that I kind of liked but overheard him telling his friends that I was cute but didn't have a body. Jerk. No worries, I had the pleasure of shooting him and all the rest of his little friends down, later once I came into my curves. I said all of this to say that even as an adult I still sometimes felt insecure and worried if I was pretty enough, or sexy enough, and it's ridiculous that it has taken me so long to realize that I AM ENOUGH. And so are you!

There's something about a woman with confidence that attracts men like crazy. Confidence is like the sexiest thing you can wear, so, when you step outside each day walk with your head held high. Try telling yourself that you're the shit and actually believe it. Be bold and daring when it comes to fashion and the way you style your hair. If you want to be a more confident person, then you have to stop standing in front of the mirror and picking yourself apart. I'm guilty of being extra hard on myself as well. Since I had my twins it has been hard to accept the fact that my body may not ever look the way it used to again. I would work out and every morning before I'd get in the shower I'd stand naked in front of the mirror and body shame myself. Then one morning I got on the scale and wasn't too pleased with the numbers and went into the shower disappointed with my results. Then suddenly something came over me and I just started to see the good in myself. I know this sounds weird but I began to talk out loud to my body. I told my body that it was amazingly strong. I thanked my body for holding it together while I carried five kids into this world. When I stepped out of the shower that day I felt stronger, happier, grateful, beautiful, and just like an overall super woman.

Try looking in the mirror and telling yourself how smart or talented you are each day. Realize you can achieve anything you put your mind to if you focus on one goal at a time and don't stop until it's done. Think of all the good things that you will have to offer that special someone one day. If you can exude confidence eventually the right person will be drawn to you and you will be perfect in their eyes.

BE A BEAUTY INSIDE AND OUT

There's no point in looking good on the outside if you're a mess on the inside. If your attitude sucks, you may want to adjust it before you go out on a quest to find a man. Try to be mindful of things like negative thinking, or complaining a lot because it's really not cute. Men don't want to date Debbie Downers, or Negative Nancies, they want girls who are fun to be around, and who can see the good in things. Haven't you ever heard that happy girls are the prettiest girls?

Sometimes people don't even realize that they are being negative and that could be part of the reason why you're still single. If you're talking to a guy and he asks how was your day, how do you reply? I hope you don't go into a long spill about how your boss got on your nerves, how badly you have cramps, or that the rain made your blowout turn frizzy. Even if your day did suck, you don't have to dwell on it or transfer that negative energy unknowingly onto him. You could reply with a simple, "It's better now that I'm talking to you. How was yours?"

Now if he continues to dig and wants to know what went wrong, then that's on him but at least you gave being positive a chance.Maybe your attitude is just OK but you are a mess on the inside because you're hurting from a previous failed relationship.Allow your heart time to heal. Get to know yourself better so that you're comfortable being single. Personally, I used to feel as if after a breakup I had to replace my ex immediately. I guess that was my way of making myself feel better. Like if I could get a new man fast, then it must've been him not me, right? Well yes who ever let me go was crazy, but maybe I was behaving like a crazy lady as well for always thinking that I needed a man to be OK. What I've learned was yes in the words of Beyoncé, 'I could have another you in a minute', but sometimes it's better to give yourself a minute and just be alone.Once you're ready to date again then go do your thing, have fun, but you have nothing to prove and there's no rush. Your flyness isn't going to wear off and you will always be amazing.

Seriously though, if you are depressed, in a funk, still carrying daddy issues, scarred from an ex, or can't get over an ex and it's been a long time, then maybe you should get counseling before dating again. There is nothing to be ashamed of and mental health is everything. Putting on makeup and looking pretty is fine but always make sure that your head is right.

And don't walk around with a bad attitude or a chip on your shoulder. Be good to people because you never know who you are dealing with, or who is watching. If you're out with a guy and you are giggling and being all sweet with him but talking to the waiter who is serving you like crap, he could stop liking you right there. To him your behavior could be a sign that you think you are better than others, or that you just aren't very nice and that's not cool. It's very important to always do a self-check and make sure your heart is just as pretty as your face. With time beauty fades so there has to be more going for you than your looks. Gravity can be cruel. Booties stop sitting so high, breasts sag, all the partying late at night gives you under eye bags. However, if you're smart and kind, or have a really big heart, those qualities tend to withstand the test of time a little bit better than some of your physical attributes. Being a good and genuine person is something that doesn't have to change as the years pass by.

I love reality television and social media because it gives platforms to people and can be entertaining to look at especially as I sip my wine late at night. But I hate the negative influence that these outlets are having on some of our younger ladies. To them, these ratchet acting, self-proclaimed bad bitches are winning. Let me tell you something, that wild behavior is not cute and if you go into public pouring drinks on people and starting fights, you're gonna go to jail! There will be repercussions and you'll more than likely regret acting such a fool later. It's just not a good look and I challenge you to be your own kind of beautiful. You don't have to always dress or act a certain way to get attention. If you strive to maintain elegance and grace you'll begin to radiate a beauty from the inside out, that is bound to catch the right type of guy's eyes. So, don't try to be too extra because you're fine just the way you are. Fake lashes, hair, or whatever enhancements you choose to use to adorn yourself with is fine, but it's that personality and inner beauty that will be the ultimate thing that can seal or break the deal. If you can balance being classy and sexy at the same time, I promise men will be intrigued by you.

BE APPROACHABLE

A friend of mines used to say that guys never try to talk to her when she's out for some reason. I didn't know what to say because she is not an ugly girl, but then one day we were meeting at the mall and I spotted her walking before she spotted me. Her face was mean and had don't bother me written all over it but I knew she was in a good mood because we had just spoke on the phone. She is not alone either, there are plenty of women who look mean but are really nice when you talk to them.

Some guys have no fear when it comes to being rejected and will try to get at any and every girl that they pass throughout the day. Then there are also men who get really nervous when it's time to approach a female or just decide not to bother her at all because they don't like being rejected. So even if a guy may find you attractive he still might not speak if you look like you don't want to be bothered. So try smiling a little more, especially if you are passing a decent looking guy and the two of you make eye contact. It doesn't cost anything to smile. And no, I'm not suggesting that you run around town grinning like Boo-boo the Fool, but be conscious of your resting bitch face, that's all. I think that a person is approachable when they are dressed nice, well groomed, and just have a friendly demeanor.

GOD BLESS THE CHILD
THAT HAS HER OWN

Some women don't have anything to offer but their good looks and they still luck up and find a man who is happy and willing to take care of them. Personally I don't understand how you can be such a choosey lover if you don't have your own pot to piss in. I believe if a woman is holding her own and taking care of herself, a man is more likely to want to take some of that load off of her shoulders, versus being with a woman who always has her hands out. That will get old quick and he is not going to want to 'help' you for long. It's not cool to be the kind of chic who just wants to see how much she can get out of a guy. Don't be that girl. When I was single, I didn't feel comfortable going on dates unless I had enough money to cover whatever it was that I wanted to do that night. I didn't offer to pay or anything, but if he lost his wallet I had us covered. Or if dude was a jerk I had money for a ride home. If you're going to be out there trying to date its good if you have yourself together. Not saying that you have to be balling but at least have your own car, your own place, and your own money. If you have yourself together, and have some sort of business about yourself you can feel good about being picky. You are established and you deserve to pick from the crème de le crème of the crop when it comes to men. Then you can be confident going into the relationship because you know that you are bringing more to the table besides a spoon and a fork. A man respects that and he wouldn't be able to throw his money or what he is doing in your face when he knows you can hold your own with or without him.

With that being said ladies, please don't cut these men too much slack! So many girls, myself included, have given guys who didn't deserve it, a chance because we think that they have potential. Don't be impressed by someone's potential! That ain't shit! A rock has potential to move but unless you pick it up and throw it it's just going to sit there! What is he doing with himself right now? I am all for couples who grind it out and grow together, I think it's beautiful and once they make it or get rich hopefully that bond remains unbreakable. However, if you are a female and you are a goal digger who is diligently working to make things happen for a brighter future, please pay attention to what steps your love interest is taking towards his goals or how he is using his God given talents. If he is going nowhere fast, then let that boy walk right on past. It's not your job to show him the way, and please don't waste your energy ever thinking you can change a guy. Listen my fellow queen, continue to focus on one goal at a time and don't stop until it's done. Most of the time the right man will find you when you are least expecting it. Like when you are so caught up in doing you that you aren't thinking of a man! Before you know it you will be complaining about not getting enough rest at night because your man is always tapping you on your shoulder trying to get some! So just continue to work on yourself and building your queendom.

Always wear your invisible crown

CLEAN UP YOUR IMAGE
ON SOCIAL MEDIA

We all know the saying be a lady in the streets and a freak in the sheets. Well I believe these days we must also mention that one should be a lady on the internet as well. Back when Myspace was popular I too was guilty of posting a raunchy picture or two, but come on now. The thirst traps are getting out of hand. Most real men don't want the whole world to be able to see their woman's goodies at the click of a button. If you want to find and keep a man, don't sell yourself short on social media by posting a bunch of half-naked, I want to be a centerfold looking pics. And you might want to think long and hard before you sext someone and send a naked picture because it could resurface on the internet one day and totally humiliate you. So, when you feel that you just have to entice a lucky guy by sending a nude, maybe it's a good idea not to include your face!

Now back to social media, if you know that you have more to offer than your body, then I believe that your social media outlets should reflect that as well. I know a lot of people meet online now so when "advertising" yourself try posting mantras that you actually live by. Or things that inspire you, and pictures of yourself having fun doing the things that you love. Don't be thirsty for likes and comments. It's not a good look to need validation from complete strangers all the time. If you don't want to attract the type of guys who only want to have sex with you then maybe you should stop only posting pictures of your ass. The way you portray yourself doesn't have to be overly sexy, be a lady on and offline.

FORGET ABOUT HAVING A PARTICULAR TYPE

When I was younger I would not entertain a guy for silly things like if he had his hair cut the wrong way! My typical type was athletic, tall, muscular, high yellow to light brown complexions, and they had to know how to dress. I mean really? After a while those type of guys began to give me headaches. I remember once I was with my ex, one day I was in the bathroom mirror talking to him while I did my hair. When he came up behind me I thought that he was admiring my beauty while listening to me talk, but when I looked up I saw that he was so into staring at his own face that he hadn't heard one word I said! I knew that we weren't going to last much longer right there because I require a lot of attention and he was just too into himself. I declared that I did not want another pretty boy. I was ready to give another type of man a try and I didn't care what he looked like anymore. Thank God my husband, James, came into my life when he did because I find him very easy on my eyes yet he doesn't act like a pretty boy. I think he is handsome, he has nice hair, and a sexy deep voice that sends chills down my spine when he whispers in my ear. He's a manly man and what I love most is that he can care less about what he looks like. Sometimes he is so busy trying to make money that he'll go days without shaving his face, the mirror is the last thing on his mind so I get it all to myself.

I always laugh because when James and I had first gotten together one day he called saying he was on my side of town with his dog so we agreed to meet at the park. When I saw him he had on this old looking white tee shirt and these too little, funky looking basketball shorts! I was so embarrassed to be seen walking with him and I could not believe he actually thought that it was ok to not only leave the house that way, but suggest to meet up with me at that! I remember walking behind him trying to take his picture so I could send it to my sister and best friend like, "Am I tripping?" This normally would have been a deal breaker for me but thank God I did not stay stuck in my shallow ways because I would have missed out on my sexy husband, his beautiful soul, and totally missed my blessing of love.

While having a type might not always be the move, I do believe that it is very important to have standards. If you are a good person then you deserve the best, so you have to implement some type of standards. You may not want to date an ex con or someone with a criminal record even if it's a misdemeanor. If you simply do not wish to entertain someone who has had run ins with the law, then no criminal record is one of your standards. Wanting a man who is financially stable is also standard for a lot of women. I am all for having reasonable standards. That means you are not going to date just anybody and that's perfectly fine. Having a type and having standards are two different things. Having a type can be a little shallow, and that's an unattractive trait to have. Having standards is great, as you should. However, I do suggest that you take a long hard look at yourself in the mirror and see yourself inside and out, and adjust your standards accordingly.

Once you set your standards do not settle. Don't lower your standards because you are lonely or just for the sake of having a man. I understand that being single can get lonely, and some of you may be worried that your biological clock is ticking and you may want to have kids. But if you settle for anything less than what your heart truly desires, you're going to be mad at yourself later. I'm sure there are some women who have settled for the wrong man because they felt pressured by their families or society to be married. I urge you not to settle for those reasons because at the end of the day it's your life and I don't want you lying awake in bed listening to your husband snore and feeling disgusted because you've let yourself down.

When it comes to guys, yes you deserve more. So, don't ever settle for a broke, no job having, multiple baby mama having, liar and or cheat. Don't even settle for a successful, faithful, boring man that doesn't give you butterflies when you see him. You want someone that you can have fun with. A man that can hold you down. A man who sends chills down your spine and makes you get all moist when he whispers in your ear! So just hold out for the perfect guy that makes you happy because good things come to those who wait.

IF HE DON'T HAVE A GOOD RELATIONSHIP WITH HIS MOM☐...RUN!!!

If your guy reveals that he does not like his mother and don't put his mother on a pedestal, then run girl run, as fast as you can! You don't want him, he won't be a good man! If a man can't love the woman who gave him life, he will never fully be able to love you. Also, remember you want a man to love his mother without being a mama's boy. There's a fine line and finding a man who has a nice healthy relationship with his mother is so special because that normally means that he knows how to treat a lady.

You've Got What He Wants

If you are out and you see a guy that you think you might like, don't you dare make that first move! When a female makes the first move I personally feel like she is giving away her power. The last thing you want to be is powerless because in the dating game some men can be quite savage. If you make it too easy he'll have his way with you and toss you to the side like some barbeque rib bones he done ate all the meat off of, and move on to the next chic because he's still hungry.

While dating, when you first start dealing with someone you have to teach them how you like to be treated, and let them know early what is or is not acceptable in your eyes. But if you were the one who initiated things, offering yourself like a free sample inside of a food court, then he is not gonna be trying to hear about your quote on quote boundaries or expectations. He might think he's exempt from the rules since after all, you wanted him, right? Wrong! You my darling are the prize and don't you ever forget it. So for Christ's sake let the man choose you!

Now when I was single there have been times where I may notice a guy, let's say at the mall, way before he sees me. Never would I approach him but I would be sure to walk his way and if we made eye contact, I'd shoot a quick smile or smize (a smile with my eyes). But I would keep moving and most of the time I'd hear him calling, "Hey Red" from behind me trying to catch up so that he could ask me out.

And if you ask him out does that mean you are paying for the date too? After all it was your idea, right? Foolishness. A real man wants to chase you, date you, and wine and dine you, so let him. If you make the first move you take all the fun out of it you risk messing with a guy who only answers your calls when he feels like being bothered because he never asked you out in the first place. Come on now, know your worth.

Never allow a man to make you feel inadequate. And please don't allow him to talk to you like he is doing you some kind of favor by being with you. There was this guy from high school who I thought was so handsome, smart, and nice. He kind of had that Denzel, I don't know I'm appealing thing going on. He was the first person I ever kissed and I was crazy about him. We didn't keep in touch or anything and he graduated a year before me. Well a few years later I saw him out and he invited me over to his place to catch up. I guess somewhere along the way he developed the big head because he sat next to me on the couch and ruined any chance he may have had in under ten minutes. He wanted me to go into his bedroom and when I said I'd rather talk on the couch, I think he got frustrated because he started to tell me how he knows he looks good and blah, blah, blah. The exact words that were used before I tuned him out were, "I know I'm fine." And he meant it!Like he turned so ugly to me in that moment that I didn't hear anything else coming out of his mouth, so I got up and left pretty much. Basically, he expected me to just give it up and it wasn't that type of party. I didn't care what he looked like, he was gonna have to earn this here. But his energy was like he was going to pull down his pants and bless me with some sort of magic stick and that I should be grateful for the opportunity. I could tell by the way he was talking that I didn't like his attitude, so I didn't waste either of our time any further. When dating, avoid any man who thinks that you should feel privileged to be by his side, because you are the trophy.He's the lucky one so don't ever get that twisted.

Dating as a Single Mom

I once read a saying that stated, it takes a strong man to accept somebody else's children and step up to the plate another man left on the table. That couldn't be more true and dating a woman with children or vice versa is not for everyone. That's why I think its best when you meet someone to let it be known as soon as possible if you have a kid or kids. Some guys might shy away while some might be like ok, when are we going to Chuck E Cheese's? If a guy does not want to pursue you any further once he finds out about your kids, don't be upset, it's his prerogative. I'm sure that both you and your little one are awesome and he is just going to miss out. Keep it pushing.

If your kids are old enough to understand things, then hopefully you have explained to them that Mommy is trying to find a husband which means you might have to go out with a few men before you find the perfect match for you and your family. Now once you've found a guy who says he doesn't mind your kids and he's still pursuing you, the next thing to do is decide when should you allow him to meet your kids. I don't suggest letting your kids meet everyone that you talk to, however being a woman who had to date with kids, I understand that it's hard to keep them away. Especially if you don't always have a babysitter. My advice, go on a few dates with the guy and if you are getting a good vibe then sure, make the next date kid friendly. That is a good chance to see how they interact with each other, and for him to see you in action dealing with the most important person in your world.

Now hanging out with your kids and possibly your new man is one thing, but please don't be a fool and leave your kids alone with a man you are just now dating and getting to know.It breaks my heart when I see stories on the news about a baby or small child who was harmed at the hands of their mother's boyfriend. Do your research on these guys, hell, check to see if he has some type of record or if he's a weird sexual predator before you trust him around your baby, your flesh and blood. Better safe than sorry.

It's a good idea not to have your kids around a bunch of different men and only introduce them to the ones you think might be special. Yes you are single and dating, but kids are not stupid and you don't want to set a bad example for them. Before James and I got married I went out of my way to keep my daughters from knowing that he would spend the night with me. We'd all hang out but when it was getting close to the girl's bedtime, I'd tell him good bye and have the girls say goodnight, and he would pretend to leave. Then he'd sneak back inside and go wait for me in my bedroom while I was still tucking them in bed. Morning would come and he'd be gone before they woke, sometimes he'd go to his house to shower and change clothes, then come back with breakfast for us all.

I'm glad that James could respect the fact that I did not want my daughters to see me laid up in bed with a man who wasn't my husband. It's a good thing that he was happy to play along because it was not up for negotiation. I was a lady, and I wanted to send a message to my little queens that not only did I have respect for myself, but I had respect for them as well and would never bring just anybody around them. And speaking of respect, I had to demand nothing less because I knew my daughters were watching. I couldn't let James get away with belittling me even if he wanted to because I did not want my daughters to see me act weak. I want my daughters to walk away from a man immediately if he talks down to them or isn't uplifting. I don't want them to tolerate any kind of foolishness because I know that they are special. Basically, I didn't want them growing up and allowing men to mistreat them because they grew up watching their mama get dogged out repeatedly, so I had to lead by example.If I did give a man the privilege to be around my daughters, his interactions with them had better been on point or else he would get cut off.

If things get serious between you and your guy, and he could possibly be a step father to your kid or kids, then it's important to tackle uncomfortable topics including discipline. The mate that you choose must be able to tolerate kids as they go through different stages growing up, and he should also be patient and caring. If you don't want your man to whoop or physically reprimand your children then that should be established early on.He needs to understand that if he puts his hands on your kid, then that will be a huge problem. As mothers, we must protect our babies, it's our duty. You have to make sure that they are always being treated fairly and that they know that you'll always have their back. Now if your mate does or says something to your kid and you're not really feeling it, I suggest you pull him to the side and address it and not do it in front of the kid(s). You wouldn't want your kid to think they don't have to listen to or respect your man. Kids might also try to walk over him if they think their mama is gonna intervene and side with them on every issue. Personally, I didn't want my husband touching my girls because I grew up with a step father who didn't hit me. I made sure my daughters knew that if they gave James a hard way to go then they would have hell to pay with me. To this day there are times where I'll check them before he even gets a chance to speak if I hear them giving him too much sass. The bottom line is everyone must give and show respect to one another if the family is going to blend smoothly.

So, to all my single ladies my advice is to go ahead and date mama, just remember that you must be extremely careful and keep in mind when choosing a mate that it's not just about you, and you should want for everyone in the situation to be happy, especially your kids.

Just Be Cool

There are ways to let a man know that you are feeling him without coming off as too desperate or thirsty. Let him breathe and don't go into a frenzy if he doesn't respond to one of your text messages right away. Take into consideration that he could be working, busy at the moment, or away from his phone. Believe it or not, not everyone walks around with their phones in their hand all day. So if you text him, be patient and wait for a response. Don't keep sending messages blowing up his spot, or assume the worst because it's just going to make you look dumb. However, if he is starting to develop a pattern of not responding to your text messages in a timely fashion, or sending your calls to voicemail, then the next time you speak you must communicate and voice your concerns to him.

Now after you have done so and you guys are newly dating, and he still doesn't change then please by all means…. fall back. This could be a sign that this guy just isn't digging you. Don't waste anymore of your time because you deserve to find that head over heels, I don't wanna be without you, Nia Long and Larenz Tate, Love Jones, kind of love.

Don't worry about looking thirsty. You aren't going to send out desperate vibes just because you call your potential guy mid-day and leave him a voice message that's simply stating that he was on your mind a little bit so you wanted to hear his voice and wish him a nice day.

You have to let on that you are into him. There is nothing wrong with that. Just don't play games and do stuff like send his call to voicemail because that's where he last sent yours. Then you spend the day playing phone tag because you decided to overthink things and act petty.

Have a life of your own and let him show you that he wants to be a part of your world. If he is into you and haven't heard from you, more than likely he will reach out to check in.

Part of being cool is also learning to live in and enjoy the moment. Stop trying to figure everything out and just go with the flow sometimes. Enjoy the dating process and don't sweat a guy or put too much pressure on him too soon because you risk taking the fun out of things.

SHUT THE F %*K UP

Sometimes we women talk way too dang on much! We go on these dates and get all nervous then start rambling and wind up putting our foots in our mouths. When you're just beginning to date and get to know a guy, during those early conversations remember that you have two ears and one mouth so you should be listening to him more and not spending all the time talking about yourself. You want to ask him fact finding questions and try to learn as much about him as possible so that you can decide if he is someone that you really want to try to take seriously and date.

What you don't want to do is start divulging too much information about yourself too soon because a man might use your words against you later. It could be the darnedest thing that he takes and store in his memory bank too. One of my old coworkers told a guy that she was dating that she had cheated on pretty much every boyfriend she ever had. After dating for a while she had problems with him because he said he didn't trust her. Maybe some of those trust issues wouldn't have arisen if she had just shut the heck up before.

Then there was another girl that I knew who had been in an abusive relationship at one point in her life. She told this new guy she was dealing with about her past. I don't know if she was looking for sympathy out of him by sharing her story or what, but what she did get was another maniac. He figured since she let her ex get away with knocking her around then he should be able to punch her when he felt like it too.

Yes, I always urge you to be open and honest when you meet a guy, but good Lord child, these men don't need to know everything right off the bat. There are so many different scenarios about women who talk too much and how it can sabotage their love lives, but I think one very important topic that you should probably stay mum on is the number of sexual partners that you've had in your life. When you are on a date vibing with a guy you are attracted to, let's say over drinks, it can be easy for the conversation to go left and the two of you start talking about sex. If you have been with a lot of men but you don't have a STD or incurable disease to prove it, then keep the amount of men you've been with to yourself! Your dude may act like it's cool and say that he will be ok with your answers but it's a lie! Most men can't handle the truth! He might have said that it wouldn't bother him but depending on your answer he might judge you. So regardless of your experience with men, don't feel obligated to answer that stupid question. You have the right to plead the fifth and change the subject.

BE GENUINE

When you are genuine, you are doing yourself the biggest favor. Nobody likes a phony. I don't know if it's because I grew up in a nice upper middle class town in Cincinnati, Ohio and attended a very diverse school, or if being genuine was just embedded inside of my DNA because my parents are good people. All I know is I am the same person no matter who I am around. And I am comfortable being myself around everyone regardless of their race, level of education, or lack of education, I am not about to lie to make myself sound better, and I will never dumb myself down to make someone else like me. To me being fake is just like being a liar and it takes entirely too much energy. One day your true colors are going to come bursting thru, so when you're getting to know a man just be yourself from the jump so that you don't risk looking wack in the end. My friend and I were just talking (being messy) about one of her so called friends the other day.She said the girl is so superficial and phony that she wasn't even using her real speaking voice while on a date with this guy. When he went to the restroom she called her talking all country and relaxed and when he returned she's like, "I gotta call you back! Hello again, handsome!" How draining. I don't know about you but I don't have time to be anything but myself and you can take it or leave it.

Games can be fun to play, but playing games with a man or while dating isn't cute. Ladies are quick to cry when we get our feelings hurt, but what about the females who make us all look bad because they simply aren't nice? If you are not genuinely into a guy and you know it, then please do not accept his gifts or take his money. And don't go out to eat with him just for a free meal either! Yes, there are some ratchet females out there who will do that unfortunately. If you don't have any intentions on being with a man, it's not cool to string him along just so that you can try to see how deep his pockets are!

I think that being genuine goes hand in hand with

being honest. It's important to be honest and not play games. When James and I were dating he pretty much knew that I was going to consider myself single and keep my options open until I could tell he was serious about trying to change my last name. I didn't lie, number one because you have to remember your lies and I have terrible memory, and number two because I wanted him to be real with me so I had to be open and honest with him no matter what.

It is so unnecessary for people to lie for no reason. If a man catches you in a lie, even a white lie, it may turn him off for good. He might not call you on it, but he is far from stupid and probably turned off for good. So if he is on to your lies and haven't said anything, it's probably because he is just trying to smash and be out at this point. You're not slick, you're not a player, depending on the lie, he might just think you're a silly hoe. It's hard to build with someone if there is no trust. Not to mention, once you tell a lie you have to keep it going and to me it's just easier to be honest about things. If the guy you are dealing with can't handle your truths, then maybe they just aren't right for you.

MAKE HIM EARN IT

So, I was talking to one of my single friends and I'm like, "Shoot, fire away with the relationship questions and I'll give you my advice." One of her questions I didn't take too serious because I'm thinking that she is old enough and she should know this already. But when she fired back with another question like but how, I knew that this topic was something that I needed to address because she is not the only girl with this concern. Her big question was, "When dating, how soon before you give it up?" My answer, once he has earned it. She then asks, "How does he earn it, with dates?" (insert sad face emoji here)

Ok ladies, I wouldn't feel right if I didn't first say that you should save yourself for marriage. That is biblical, and being able to abstain from sex until marriage is also very noble. I salute any female who successfully abstained until wedding vows were exchanged. Kudos. I would want that for my daughters.

Now let's be realistic. With our over sexualized culture, people these days just aren't waiting to have sex. Some people believe the whole ninety-day thing is a good rule. I personally see room for error if you enter a new relationship announcing that he must wait ninety days for a chance to get some. A real creep could go mark the days off his calendar and act like the perfect gentleman until the ninety days are up and he has gotten what he wants. Then on that ninety first day, he is nowhere to be found. Or he could be having sex with side chicks pretending to wait with you because he likes having you as his challenge.

So, going into everything with this number of days in your head that must be spent before the two of you can get it in just makes it weird to me. Even though I'm sure it has worked for a lot of people. Every situation is different and a relationship is not some cookie cutter thing. You can't expect what worked for Jack and Jill to work for Tyrone and Sharmaine. Just do you and don't worry about the opinions of others because what works in your relationship may not work for them.

I think waiting until he has earned your good love is the best way to go because if you believe that he's earned it then more than likely you've gotten something you wanted out of the deal and if the relationship goes awry afterwards then you won't be so upset and can still walk away with a little bit of dignity. The last thing you want is to feel used and have to get mad every time you hear his name or think about what the two of you had shared.

Giving it up too easily is the fastest way to not get taken seriously by a guy. The late great Tupac Shakur said a mouthful on his track, 'I Get Around' when he said:

And every time she sees me, she squeeze

me, lady take it easy

Hate to sound sleazy, but tease me, I don't

want it if it's that easy

Gosh I was thirteen years old when that song was released and come to think of it as much as I heard my brother playing it, and constantly hearing the song on the radio, I think Tupac may have had a hand in me not growing up to be a hoe! His words stuck with me, so thanks Pac!

And I'm not saying that a relationship can't spawn off a one night stand. Sometimes you just get a feeling that shoots thru you when you meet someone and you just know that you've got to have them. I'm talking soul connection type of vibes. But that's rare so if you want him to love you and plan a future with you, then wait to be intimate until you feel that he is emotionally invested. It's not the number of dates the two of you have gone on, it's about the time he has invested in pursuing you, and the connection. Yes, we all want a man with money who is secure financially, but earning your body shouldn't be about money spent on dates or anything like that because you're a valuable woman and it's hard to put a price on you.

***************So You've Found One******

Keeping a Man
THE DOUBLE F METHOD

W hen James and I were dating he told me to keep him happy just remember the two F's. Feed me, Fuck me. Not too hard. I figured that was a fair request. If you're doing those two things well, then you're already ahead of the game. If only it were that simple, I'd end the book right now. Boom. You're welcome, have a great love life. But no my friend, it's going to take a little more effort on your part if you're in it for the long haul. What I'm about to say might get some feminist worked up, but if you're trying to secure your spot on his team then grab a highlighter and let this sink in.

When I was a little girl in school they taught us about the basic needs of life. Well a relationship has basic needs as well. By feeding and fucking your man you are only meeting the basic needs. Those two things should be automatic. Even if you guys are mad. Fuck your frustrations out. I promise that's my last time dropping the f bomb. I'm not Potty Mouth Patty, I'm just trying to get a point across and we're all adults here. So to avoid the F bomb, let's call it the Double F Method.

On top of the Double F Method you have to be loyal and compassionate because as hard or tough as our men are, they have feelings too. They often carry the weight of the world on their shoulders but don't complain out loud. So when you man comes home after a long day, try not making everything about you and how your day went, and just start taking off his clothes to relieve some of that stress for him. Ask how his day went as you're kissing his neck and getting ready to ride him or something. Just remember you are not being a five-star chick for your man if you haven't even mastered the Double F Method. So go take a cooking class or two, learn some recipes off of the Food Network on TV or something, and then go pick up a Kama Sutra book and remember to always keep it spicy.

BE HIS LITTLE FREAK

You would think that after a certain age I wouldn't have to tell women how to keep it spicy for their men. You'd actually be surprised how many women think they are pleasing their man because they give him a little lazy sideways or missionary loving a few times a week. Some women don't realize that in order to keep your man you should be doing all the things that got him hooked in the first place!

Come on ladies, how many of you are guilty of giving you man mind blowing brain when you were dating but have since reduced his oral transactions to his birthday or special occasions? Tisk, tisk, tisk! I don't care if you guys are mad at each other; head is always welcome! Never in my life have I heard a man say, "No you cannot suck my dick, Tiana!" I'm sorry but it's true. And trust me I know it's something that some women absolutely dread. I have a friend who hates it because pre cum grosses her out. Another friend of mine would complain that her jaws always get tired. These excuses sound funny but it's not a laughing matter when you find out that your man has been creeping on his lunch breaks with Becky with the good hair because she likes to go down on him.

As far as those tired jaws, the whole process could be quicker if you get into it and put in more work. I know that I personally have a short attention span and after five minutes of bobbing I'm usually over it. So I did some homework which included watching videos, asking questions, and practice. Now I can get things done quickly, he's in a good mood, everybody's happy and I can go about my business.

Sometimes I cheat and use props during oral sex too. Take a trip to your local adult novelty store and ask what items they have to make oral more pleasurable for both parties. I've learned the wetter the better, so one of my favorite items are these little wet mouth candies. The hard candies cause your mouth to get really wet by helping you to produce more saliva so that you can really spit all over his joy stick!

There are also different sleeves you can buy to slide

over the penis that will heighten pleasure and assist with hand jobs. The two things I've just mentioned are some inexpensive items that can help you take your man to ecstasy rather quickly. And I know that I joke and talk about getting it done fast but that's because we have a lot of kids who are likely to interrupt our groove at any given time. My James understands that so we are on the same page. Sometimes we just want to hurry up and bust a nut. But don't rush everything all of the time! It's also very important not to treat going down on your man as if it is a chore. He would probably enjoy it more if it seems like you enjoy what you're doing and you're actually getting pleasure by pleasing him.

In order to be his little freak you must be willing to lose your inhibitions and not be afraid to try new things, or to scream out loud! Tell him what you like while he's doing it, and allow yourself to be totally engulfed in the moment. The best orgasms are reached when you are able to tune everything out, clear your mind and focus completely on what's happening and just feel your man with your mind, body, and soul.

DON'T SEEK ADVICE FROM YOUR SINGLE FRIENDS

My oldest two kids aren't my husband's biological daughters. So when we first got married and he felt it was ok to walk around in his drawls, I freaked out. I thought it was super inappropriate and he didn't feel like it was a big deal. We kept having little fights about it. I wanted to know if I was just tripping or overreacting. I did not want to ask my mom who is like my best friend, because I didn't want her all up in our new marriage mix. Then I was going to ask some of my girlfriends that I spoke to everyday, but I got to thinking, "They don't even have men so why should I bring this to them?" Thank goodness, I remembered a good old friend I went to high school with who had been married to her husband for a while. I sent her a message on Facebook and she gave me some good sound advice that really helped. She also said she was glad that I had sense to ask a married friend because our single friends would get us caught up every time.

This may sting a little but if you don't have a man, you know, a nice warm body in your bed every night, then it ain't nothing you can tell me when it comes to mine! I'm sorry if that's offensive but to me it's just not logical.

DON'T LET PRIDE BLOCK YOUR BLESSINGS

‹or my ladies who are still dating, are you independent? Great! That's wonderful and all but you still have to let him help you. If he asked to take you out, let him pay for the meal. It's part of allowing him to be the man. Let's say you're still technically single and even though you worked overtime last week, you're still short on your rent. Don't suffer and stress in silence because you don't want him to think you're a bum chic. If he's a good guy, into you, with extra money, I'm sure he'd be happy to save the day for you. So don't let pride block your blessing. But if you always have your hand out and expect guys to just give you things all of the time, then you should be ashamed of yourself and figure out how to become a go getter and get your own.

Having too much pride can mess you up and really suck the life out of your relationship. I know people who are currently walking around feeling like their main ingredient is missing because their pride caused them to lose someone that they really cared for. Let's say that you are into it with your mate. You each feel that the other was wrong in the situation and maybe some words were said on both ends that probably should not have been spoken. Don't be afraid to say I'm sorry first. Apologizing first doesn't cause you to lose any type of leverage or anything. Apologizing first is simply a way for the two of you to get out of your feelings and make up, no longer wasting time being angry. I don't care if you're married or single, if you love someone and know deep down that this fight isn't the end, then why prolong it? Neither one of you are going anywhere so send your pride packing and go make nice with your bae.

Pride will sometimes cause you not to accept an apology as well. Cut it out. Accept his apology before he takes it back already! Recognize and be grateful that you are dealing with someone who gives enough of a fuck about you to admit when they are wrong and at least try to make it right. Now if he is always freaking sorry about something, then that's totally different. If he is always letting you down then by all means, allow him to go and be sorry somewhere else.

Don't be too proud to admit when you're hurting. If your guy said or did something that hurt your feelings, ditch the tough act and for God's sake do not waste time on the silent treatment! You should communicate because no matter how awesome your man is, he is not a mind reader. Often times people, especially guys, have no idea that their actions were offensive and will go on their merry little way while you're sitting somewhere mad. So, you can't be too proud to open your mouth and say, "Yes, I'm in my feelings because when you did (blank), I felt (blank)."

It's also very important to keep pride out of your bedroom. Well to an extent, personally I'm not about to let my man spit on me or do any crazy weird mess. I'm saying push pride aside when it comes to keeping love alive. Trying to keep the thrill in a relationship or marriage can be challenging at times.

A while back my husband and I were in a little sexual funk. For some reason (mainly kids and his 60 plus hours a week work schedule), our sex life had taken a horrific turn for the worse. We hadn't kissed, we hadn't cuddled, and when we finally tried to make time for sex it was awkward and forced and he walked away with blue balls while I went to bed pissed. We weren't satisfying each other and I felt unsexy and sad.Am I not sexy anymore? I know my body isn't the same after the babies, maybe I need vaginoplasty? He's not really working all those hours, he cheating! All kinds of different thoughts started going thru my mind. The old me would have wanted to go out and see if I still had it, if other men still found me desirable, or if my coochie really was broken! But since I love my husband I put my pride aside and just tried. Even though I had nowhere to go I did my hair and makeup. I also put on a cute little dress with some heels and waited until he came home from work. I looked better and was in a better mood that evening and when he saw me he was a little confused at first but overall pleasantly surprised. Normally I'm wearing one of his oversized t-shirts with no makeup and messy hair. Anyway, my efforts didn't go unnoticed and that night it went down, we both went to sleep happy, and we've been good ever since.

The take away from that story should be, when

the spark begins to die down, don't get defensive or cocky. Don't go outside of your union to try and make sure you're still 'fly'. Swallow your pride, take a big gulp, and simply try. Put on something sexy even if you're not feeling his ass. Try to kiss him, let him get it in his favorite position. If it's not reciprocated or it doesn't work, then maybe seek out some professional help. But if you love your mate you cannot let that flame burn out, period. Also, my friend, know when to fold 'em. In the words of Rob Base, "It takes two to make a thing go right." You can't be over there swallowing pride until you drown while your guy is making little to no effort at all. It's a two-way street and hopefully you both kick pride to the curb.

Keeping a man
SOLVE PROBLEMS
WITH LOVE

So often couples get into fights or disagreements and immediately start hitting below the belt verbally. Emphasis on verbally because if things get physical on either end then throw in the towel immediately. I had to learn the hard way in a previous relationship that you should have zero tolerance for any form of physical violence. No second chances.

Anyway, if you and your mate are having a disagreement and things are getting heated…...walk away. Go for a ride, go in the other room, just allow yourself a moment to settle down and gather your thoughts so that you don't blurt something hurtful out of anger. When James and I first got together he would just get quiet if we were about to have an altercation. Let me tell you, his silence or him walking out the door would piss me off to the highest level of pisstivity! I wanted to fight and I didn't know how to handle him walking away and returning with flowers! What the hell was that? That man saved me and really taught me how to love again I swear.

By backing up and giving each other space it gave both of us time to cool off and gather our thoughts, which was a good thing. I now try to be more aware, and sort of taste my own words before they come off of my tongue. Verbal scars take longer to heal and the last thing you want is to hurt or scar the one that you love. Try not to yell because often times when you yell your mate is still not hearing you because they shut down or go into defense mode. If a person is being yelled at they feel as if they are being attacked. So go ahead and get into a shouting match if you want to but I bet you both walk away with a headache and a problem that's not solved.

Love is patient, love is kind, so even when you are angry you have to remember to try to solve problems that arise with love. This may sound easier said than done when you're upset but it's really not that hard when you truly care for someone.

When my husband and I fight we never take it too far. Even upset we remember our boundaries, because at the end of the day we exchanged vows in front of God, in front of our closest friends and family, and we are not separating until death do us part, dang it! It can be a fight over finances, parenting disagreements, whatever. Big or small, I'm not going anywhere and neither is he, so go be mad and take a little breather. Then let's come back cool, calm, and collected and work this thing out using love.

Proverbs 18:21 mentions death and life are in the power of the tongue. I love my husband and even angry I don't want to see him hurting. I might wanna say something to shut him up at the moment, but I remember to watch what I say. I want to speak life, prosperity, and peace into my marriage and my man. I don't want to use my tongue to tear him down or cause him pain. I think its very important to choose your words wisely because once you spit that venom out of your mouth you cannot take it back.

Luckily James is pretty conscious about the things he says to me as well. I love the fact that after all of our years together and all of our heated arguments, he has never called me a bitch. Why would he if I'm his queen? So even angry he is very good about watching his mouth. Using love isn't something you should try to do only during arguments. In your relationship you should use love with whatever you do. In fact, I believe that was some of the best advice my step father gave us during our wedding reception. His voice still resonates in my mind to this day saying, "No matter what you do, do it with love." Before you do things you should always think about how it will make your partner feel.

I use love when I'm cooking dinner for my family. There are seven of us and sometimes a lot is going on while I'm standing over the stove trying to cook but I smile and my heart is warm because I count my blessings. I'm happy to have five smart, healthy kids to feed, who are growing each day. I'm grateful that we are able to put food on the table for them all. I think about my husband walking in the door from work all tired and hungry, and how much better he feels when he finishes his plate and kick his feet up in front of the TV. Thoughts like that are what motivates me while I'm cooking so that extra little ingredient that I like to add to my food that no one can quite put their finger on, is love.

Try not to Nag

What's the first thing you say to your man when you wake up in the morning? If it's anything other than, "Good morning, babe" or something along those lines then you need to get your life as Tamar Braxton would say. There should be no nagging early in the morning. Men hate to be nagged at any time of the day I'm sure, but especially when they first wake up. I understand that sometimes nags really do mean well, I get it. But if there is a task you're worried about, trust in the man that you chose to do what needs to be done on his own. He doesn't need you riding his back or all of your nagging in his ear. Being a nag isn't cute and when someone nags me it makes me want to do the opposite of what they're asking of me, so I could imagine how irritating nagging is for a man.

Have you ever gone on and on until your man said, "You sound like my mom, damn!" Well if you have don't make a habit out of working his nerves like that because no man wants his woman to remind him of the most annoying trait he had to deal with out of his mother while growing up.

Often our men keep quiet although there is a lot on their minds that they are dealing with. Your home should be a safe place and when he gets home from work he should be able to finally exhale and kick his feet up while his worries from the day fade away. No man wants to have to hear his nagging woman's voice in their ear when they are just trying to unwind. If your man is pulling into the driveway after a long day and finds himself just sitting in the car for another twenty minutes drinking a beer and dreading the idea of walking through the front door, then that's a problem. Now if your guy just so happens to like his little me time alone in the car, then that's different. But you nagging little ladies know exactly who you are and should try not to worry your man to death because you might push him into the arms of another woman who happens to be more carefree and fun to be around. I'm just saying.

LET HIM LEAD

I know some feminist might have a problem with me saying a woman should let the man lead, but if you don't want to be alone forever, then you might want to give it a try. In the relationship I had before my husband, I was the oldest and my ex wasn't very assertive so I pretty much called all the shots. I think by doing so he really resented me for it. I'm not even a bossy person, I just took the control because it was obvious that he still had some growing up to do and I pretty much had it all figured out. At least I thought. Clearly that relationship didn't last and when I began dating James, I jokingly said one day that he should just let me wear the pants. He was like, "Hell no!" He couldn't believe that I even suggested something like that. To this day he won't let me live that comment down. James is a manly, take charge kind of man.

His good work ethic and his actions made me feel comfortable enough to sit back and let him lead. When you let your man lead its less that you have to deal with anyway.

It's also very important for a man to feel like a man. So once its established that he has his head on straight and he is fully capable of leading you and your family in the right direction and not into brick walls, then by all means…... let him have at it!

Once I realized my man enjoyed leading so much I fell all the way back. I let him lead the way, especially to the bank to drop those deposits (wink). I love my dainty role at home. And don't get it twisted, I speak my mind and he respects my opinion. I just refrain from challenging him or his decisions in front of our kids or certain others. When you allow your man to lead you are saying, "I trust you. I trust you with my heart, I trust you with my life, and I trust in the man that you are and the positive path that you are on during this journey we call life."

So yes, I do let my man wear the pants in our relationship. I don't need to wear the pants anymore because I've realized that a nice pretty dress looks way better on me anyway.

BE APPRECIATIVE

I t's a well-known fact that no one likes to feel unappreciated. If your man feels appreciated he's going to want to do so much more to put or keep a smile on your face. If you are hard to please or your guy thinks that you are never satisfied, then eventually he may just give up because he feels that there's nothing he can do to make you happy. He is going to feel like his efforts aren't good enough and you don't want him to stop trying or stop caring.

Men carry a lot of weight on their shoulders, so every now and then just let him know, "I see you. I appreciate you."

You can express your appreciation verbally or you can get creative with your actions and show him how thoughtful you are. Of course an obvious way to show your appreciation could take place in the bedroom. (There is no wonder I have five kids, I use sex as a solution to just about everything)

But seriously, say he has had a long day and comes home and pretty much goes straight to bed. Try showing him that you appreciate all the hard work he does by following him to the bedroom, hopping on top of him, and putting him to sleep

Another way to remind your man that he is appreciated is to tell him so by jotting down a quick message on a post it note. I found some really cute lip shaped post its once and every now and then I'd write, "Thanks for being a hard worker!" "Hey babe, hope you have a great day," Or just a simple "I love you" and stick it on his steering wheel so that he sees it as soon as he gets in his car on the way to work.

The most obvious yet often forgotten way to show your appreciation is to simply say, "Thank you." Remembering to say thank you is so important. After a while you can sometimes develop an attitude like your man is just supposed to do certain things and they are expected. But at the end of the day no one has to do anything so remember to mind your manners that you learned early on as a kid. A thank you really means a lot sometimes. For example, I've been a licensed cosmetologist for years now so I can pretty much style my daughters hair anyway they ask me to. Sometimes I feel as if they take me for granted. There are days where they expect me to style it over because they don't like a certain detail. Well the other day as I finished giving my oldest daughter the spa treatment, she said, "Thanks for fixing my hair" as she walked away, and it took me completely off guard. It made me feel good and glad that I took the time out of my day to get it done.

If you are sincere and truly grateful, showing your appreciation should happen automatically. Once when James and I were still dating he got me a dozen roses just because. A few days later he was coming over my house after he got off work and I knew the flowers wouldn't last much longer so I filled my foot bath with water and placed some of the rose petals inside. I also lit candles all around the room and had soft music playing. I did my hair and makeup, and put on a sexy corset with a matching thong and some heels.

When he came inside I took him by the hand and led him to his seat, got on my knees, and gave him a relaxing pedicure and foot massage. The same roses he gave to me that made me feel special, loved, and appreciated, were floating around his feet as I told him thanks again in my own little way. He was so pleased with me that day that I swear I got my engagement ring shortly after that. So remember to show your mate some appreciation and it will definitely keep things running smoothly in your relationship.

COMPROMISE

If you're not the type who is ever really willing to compromise, you know, bend a little, then maybe you're the type who should just stay single and be happy. In a relationship, you must be willing to meet each other halfway if you want things to work. When it comes to compromising, it doesn't have to be some huge dilemma either, it could be something as small as where you're going for dinner. But if you never compromise and always have to have your way...it could wear heavy on a relationship.

My husband has a motorcycle. I hate it. I don't like smelling like outside when I get to where I'm going, the helmet messes up my hair, and I feel as if I'm risking my life whenever I get on it. But he loves to ride and will do it any chance he gets.One Saturday morning I wanted to go climb Stone Mountain for exercise and I wanted him to come but I could tell that he wasn't too pumped about going. On our way to the door I grabbed my pink helmet and his whole face lit up because I never want to ride. We ended up having a smooth ride, and a great morning that set the tone for our whole day and remainder of the weekend.

Big or small you may not always get your way but the more flexible you are as a couple, the smoother the sailing will be. Being willing to compromise and being dedicated to keeping each other happy is key.

"Love is ever evolving and it takes compromise, work, and patience" wise words from Jessica Alba.

KEEP YOUR PROBLEMS TO YOURSELF

We all need to vent sometimes. I get it, trust me I do. But you have to be careful who you vent to and how frequently you are venting to that person. If you are constantly complaining about your man to your best friend, eventually she might start to feel a certain way about him. If you have a close friend she is not going to be a big fan of someone who is constantly upsetting her BFF.

If your mate does something to you or has done something that you don't like, give yourself time to sort through your feelings. Don't be so quick to call your friends and family to tell them all about your troubles. Out of love you may get over it and forgive your mate but others won't. They are not in love with your spouse so depending on what the problem was, he may just very well stay on their shit list for a long time.

For instance, say I'm your BFF and you tell me that you have fallen for a guy named Johnny. Then you call me up crying saying that you caught Johnny cheating and instead of apologizing, he got mad at the fact that he was caught and bust you upside your head or blacked your eye. Naturally I'm going to be furious with this Johnny guy, so two weeks later when you're back swooning over him I'm going to still be mad. I will have no other choice but to assume that you both are crazy now. And it's going to be awkward if we are all at the same get together or something because I'm not going to want to be around him. Then you'll start to feel torn between your best friend and your man, and it's just a big mess that could have been avoided.

So maybe that was an extreme example. Maybe you find yourself complaining to your mom about your husband every day because he never helps around the house or with the kids. Mother is not gonna be very pleased with the thought that her little girl is being taken for granted or treated unfairly. If you keep on sharing every little negative thing he's doing, and never mention the good, chances are your mom is going to begin to dislike your husband.

My advice, if you want your family and friends to remain fond of your mate, then refrain from dragging his name through the mud to them just because you're upset. Don't go getting on Facebook or social media and start posting subliminal relationship shots, or going on rants. That just make others feel uncomfortable, upsets your man, or give people who were rooting for you guys to fall a reason to smile. Instead try writing your thoughts down in a journal or diary to make yourself feel better. If what you write is really mean then maybe write it down on a piece of notebook paper and when you're done rip it up so that no one finds it. Whatever you do just limit sharing your man's dirty dog way until you are fed up. But hopefully you won't entertain a dirty dog, especially not for long because we're queens, right? We deserve the best and don't you forget it.

THE SECRET

A re you ready? Lean in and pay close attention. The secret to keeping your man is to continue to do all of the things that you did that made him fall for you in the first place! If you were really in shape and into fitness when you first got together, you should not be allowed to let yourself go and get fat. It's not fair. I'm sure he loves you unconditionally but my God, don't take advantage of his heart! Men are visual creatures and I'm sure he would love to see your body at its best. I understand things change and gravity pulls at places you weren't expecting it to tug at. Booty's don't sit as high, and boobies may hang low. Just like a man may go bald or cant "perform" the way he used to when he was twenty years old. We are human, but if you make a conscious effort to stay in shape, do your squats and workout, I'm sure your man would be happy. On top of looking good, being fit will increase your chances of living longer which means the more time you'll have here on earth to love on your man.

If you used to dress nice all the time when the two of you were dating, then don't get comfortable and start walking around looking a mess. I know that this is hard, especially when you have small kids. I have been guilty of running errands in my husband's oversized sweatshirt and some sweats. And it's not good because you never know who you are going to run into, especially here in Atlanta. I remember running into Porsche from the Real Housewives Of Atlanta at Frederick's of Hollywood once when I was shopping for some lingerie for an anniversary video I was making for James. Everyone who knows me can tell you that at the time I loved her to death and wanted to be in the "circle". But there was no way in hell I could speak while I was looking like a ragamuffin. That day was kind of a reality check for me, I realized that I was getting way too comfortable with looking any old kind of way. Because I was a stay at home mom I felt like I didn't have a reason to get jazzy anymore. That was the furthest from the truth. I figured that if not for myself then my husband is all the reason I need to get dolled up every day. I'm not saying that you have to have your face beat for the Gods at all times, but make sure you are showered with your hair styled nice. The least you could do is put some mascara and lip gloss on your face before your man comes home from work.

I am a firm believer of if you look good, you feel good. So throw away the oversized tees and sweatshirts. And don't try to hold onto those funky looking favorite pants that you've washed a thousand times. You know the pants with the whole hole on your inner thigh or between your legs...just let them go! The next time you have to run errands or go on play dates, or if you're just doing laundry while waiting for your man to get off work, try putting on a nice little fitted tee, some jeans, and a few accessories. Victoria Secret jogging suits are an easy go to look for running errands as well. Wear whatever you like but no more oversized unflattering clothes. It's not cute. And if you look in the mirror and see you are looking good, I guarantee it will help your attitude, you will feel prettier, more confident, and even sexier.

So if the secret to keeping your man is doing what you did to get him, then for those who did not wait for marriage or a commitment to become his little freak, then don't stop now. Not to be repetitive but I cannot reiterate the importance of keeping your man sexually satisfied enough. If you started out going full throttle with him, you know just ready whenever, wherever, now that he's committed to you is not the time to slow down.Don't become a lackadaisical lover in the bed. Try not to just lay there even if you are tired. With as many kids as I have, I know what it is to be dog tired by the time you get in the bed at night. There have been times where I'd pray that James was too tired to want to get it on as well, but that rarely happens. So from experience I can tell you that if you just push through it (just like a workout at the gym) you will get into it and actually be glad that you did once it's over.

You have to keep your man's mind blown by doing things he doesn't expect. One time I was at the grocery store shopping a few days after Valentine's day and saw this red apron with white hearts all over it. Since the holiday had passed the apron was marked down for like two bucks. A light bulb immediately went off in my head so I bought it of course. The next morning I got out of bed before James and when he finally made his way into the kitchen, there I was making his breakfast wearing nothing but that apron and a pair of red heels that I knew he always loved to see me in. Needless to say he was not expecting that and wore a smile on his face all day.

It's easy to keep your man satisfied if you don't hold out in the bedroom.Always try to think of a way to spice things up, and don't be afraid to try something new. And try not to give all of you and your positive energy to people outside the home like coworkers, strangers, the clerk at the grocery store, and then come home and barely give your mate a smile or a listening ear. It's not just a sexual thing, show your spouse some enthusiasm, muster up some energy after a long day to make him feel special. Even if it's just staying up thirty minutes later to watch his favorite TV show with him.

Don't Quit

If you truly want your relationship to last then its simple, don't quit. You just cannot quit and I'm talking about when the two of you haven't been vibing for weeks and you can't seem to remember why you even agreed to marry this dude in the first place because he gets on your freaking nerves! Don't quit. Pull out some old photos from when your relationship was young, or if you're married then watch your wedding video and remember the way you felt that day. As a couple, you can't stop trying to make each other happy. Always remember that no relationship is perfect and you simply can't give up on your love no matter what. If you are married then I'm going to need you to go ahead and remove the word "divorce" from your vocabulary. Divorce is not the answer and it should not be used as a threat in every argument either. No one's divorcing anyone because quitting just isn't an option. Period.

Every person has their own breaking point or ultimate no no's and if their mate commits one of those no no's, then the relationship or marriage is a wrap. It's going to be over with no further discussion and no amount of begging or pleading from your mate would be enough to stop you from walking away. My husband knows that I have two things that will make me walk away. I will not tolerate any type of abuse, and I will not tolerate infidelity. If he cheats then it better be worth it because if I find out, I'm gone. But other than those two things, depending on the circumstance I'm going to tough things out with my man because my marriage isn't something that I look at as being easily disposed of.

Don't be surprised it there are times where you don't even like your spouse very much. You might find yourself wondering if you made the right decision by getting with him. Maybe you find yourself missing the single life and you just want to throw in the towel. Don't. Keep loving your man. Keep seeing the good in him and don't spend too much energy focusing on the bad. Remember we are all human and make mistakes. Don't think about the single life that you left behind because it's gone, it's the past. The present life you currently share with your man is a gift, so be grateful that you've found a good one while so many others are still searching.

If you have not familiarized yourself with the 80/20 rule of relationships then google it. It's about throwing away eighty percent of your joy for twenty percent of pleasure that you think you're missing. I think that the whole concept is good because it can help people put things relationship wise into perspective and stop picking their partners apart so much.

I could tell you to remember things like the grass isn't greener on the other side, or a bunch of other sayings that are so cliché, but you're gonna do what you want to do at the end of the day so I'll just suggest one thing. Focus on your own love life and don't pay attention to what's going on to your left, right, or behind you even. Don't waste energy dwelling on would have, could have, or should haves, and just appreciate what you have. If you nurture your relationship and pay it proper attention, over the years it will continue to blossom into a special kind of love.

Hopefully You've read something in this guidebook that will stick with you and help you in your love life. If you have a good man in your life then hold on to him tight. There are women out there praying for the type of man that you could be taking for granted. Do everything in your power to please him and make the relationship work and I'm sure your efforts will be reciprocated.

To all my single ladies, you've got this! When you leave the house each day stay optimistic. Don't say stuff like "I won't ever find a man," or "All of the good men are taken."Instead try telling yourself that it's raining men and be open to giving love a try. Best of luck!

Love,
Tiana

LOVE.NEVER.FAILS.

Acknowledgements

I have to thank God first and foremost for giving me this talent to express myself through words. I'm grateful for my life and this journey so far.

I have to thank my mother. Without her of course I wouldn't be here. From a young age my mother would tell me what not to take from a man and to always remember that I was the prize. She taught me so much and I love her for that. Thanks Mommy for giving me so much game and building up my self-esteem.

Thanks to my kids for unknowingly being my motivation. Thanks for keeping yourselves busy around the house while I was writing this book. Mommy wasn't trying to ignore you, just trying to finish a project that meant a lot to me. I wanted to show you guys that you can do anything you put your mind to.

And last but not least, I must thank my husband. Thank you for all the love and support that you pour into me on a daily basis. Thank you for being a standup guy, a good father, and a great lover. You seriously restored my faith in men. Thanks for actually seeing me and not being like all the other guys. You're my best friend and my heart is forever yours.